BRITISH MILITARY AVIATION

1960s in colour

No.1
Meteor / Valiant / Beverley

BRITISH MILITARY AVIATION

1960s in colour

No.1
Meteor / Valiant / Beverley

MARTIN DERRY

DALRYMPLE
& VERDUN◆
PUBLISHING

**British Military Aviation
No 1: Gloster and
Armstrong-Whitworth Meteor
Vickers Valiant and Blackburn Beverley**
Martin Derry

ISBN 978-1-905414-09-3

First published in 2007 by
Dalrymple & Verdun Publishing
33 Adelaide Street, Stamford,
Lincolnshire PE9 2EN
Tel: 0845 838 1940
mail@dvpublishing.co.uk
www.dvpublishing.co.uk

Printed in England by
Ian Allan Printing Ltd
Riverdene Business Park
Molesey Road, Hersham, Surrey
KT12 4RG

Half title: Valiant BK.1, XD866,
Hucknall, 3rd June 1963. Delivered
to the RAF in March 1957, this
aircraft joined 138 Squadron before
being allocated to 232 OCU, which
had formed in 1954 at Gaydon to
provide operational training for
Valiant crews. XD866 was serving
with 232 OCU at this time and was
scrapped at Marham during 1965.

Title page: A formation of three
Meteor F.8s of the RAFCAW at RAF
Manby, Lincolnshire on an unknown
date. The aircraft are WL161 'D',
WK655 'B' and WK876 'A'.

Opposite page: Beverley XL131 ' L',
47 Squadron, RAF Finningley,
September 1965. The 47 Squadron
motif seen on the tail fin depicts a
demoiselle crane's head as featured
on the Squadron Badge and
indicates the Squadron's service in
the Sudan, close to the Nile where
the crane lives. The crane's head is
superimposed on a fountain that
commemorates an earlier
amphibious role, possibly recalling
the use of floatplanes to patrol
sections of the Upper Nile during
the inter-war period.

CONTENTS

RAF unit abbreviations

A&AEE	Aeroplane & Armament Experimental Establishment
AFS	Advanced Flying School
ANS	Air Navigation School
APC	Armament Practice Camp
APS	Armament Practice Station
BAC	British Aircraft Corporation
BCCS	Bomber Command Communication Squadron
BCDU	Bomber Command Development Unit
CAACU	Civilian Anti-Aircraft Co-operation Unit
CFE	Central Fighter Establishment
CFS	Central Flying School
CSE	Central Signals Establishment
ECM	Electronic Counter Measures
ETPS	Empire Test Pilots School
FTS	Flying Training School
ITS	Instrument Training Squadron
MoS	Ministry of Supply
MU	Maintenance Unit
OCU	Operational Conversion Unit
RAE	Royal Aircraft Establishment (Royal Aerospace Establishment from 1st April 1988)
RAFCAW	Royal Air Force College of Air Warfare
RAFFC	Royal Air Force Flying College
RAuxAF	Royal Auxiliary Air Force
SoTT	School of Technical Training
THUM Flt	Temperature and HUMidity Flight
TT	Target Tug

A flavour of the past for enthusiasts and inspirational images for the modeller

This title is the first in a projected series of six or more books intended to make available to enthusiasts and modellers alike, a collection of 35mm colour images covering British military aircraft, the vast majority of which have rarely, if ever, been published before. The photographs were taken chiefly in the 1960s, however, several date from the mid-1950s of which a minority have had to be restored following some deterioration, although the remainder have survived in good condition.

Military aviation 40 or 50 years ago was as colourful as it was varied and so, it is hoped, this series will deliver both a flavour of the past and create a sense of nostalgia for the enthusiast who remembers those days, or, be of interest to those too young to recall them with clarity, or even at all!

This series will employ a loose theme in presenting at least three aircraft categories per volume, once classed as fighter, bomber, transport or training aircraft etc. The intention is to avoid an amorphous collection of images by adding diversity and where possible, despite the contradiction, a small selection of visiting foreign military aircraft will be included.

It should perhaps be stated at this point that this series is not intended to offer a full development or operational history of any given type of aircraft; space precludes that – although an introduction is provided for each type. Wherever possible dates and locations are given with each image used, though unfortunately, some images are without either, their original notes being sadly incomplete. Should any reader feel able therefore to supply information regarding these gaps, I would be only to pleased to hear from them – via the publisher; such information could be included in later works as an addendum.

All of the images reproduced in this series (unless otherwise indicated) are courtesy of the Newark Air Museum, located at Winthorpe in Nottinghamshire. I would like to express my own and the publishers gratitude to all of the members of the museum staff for their courtesy and assistance, and especially to the curator Mike Smith, for granting the author access to his valuable time, knowledge and resources over many months. I would also like to thank Chris Salter for his invaluable contribution.

Martin Derry, October 2007.

Opposite: Meteor F.8 WH291, date and location unknown. This aircraft appears again on page 16.

Gloster/Armstrong-Whitworth Meteor

Designed by the Gloster Aircraft Company, the Meteor was the first jet aircraft to enter squadron service with the RAF and indeed, was the first British jet fighter to fly; the first production Meteor F.I, EE210, flew for the first time in January 1944. Just 20 of this mark were built, as remaining production was transferred to later models, however, despite the small number constructed enough existed for several to be allocated to 616 Squadron in July 1944, thereby becoming both Britain's and the Allies' first operational jet squadron.

The performance of the F.I was barely adequate, offering little if any speed advantage at medium and high altitudes over the latest piston-engined fighters; although at low altitude the Meteor's speed performance was impressive, being capable of achieving approximately 450 mph in level flight. The F.I was replaced on the production line by the F.III with over ten times as many being built as the F.I, the first examples to be received by the RAF were also allocated to 616 Squadron in January 1945. The F.III possessed more powerful engines than its predecessor conferring a superior performance over, not just the F.I, but its piston-engined contemporaries as well, and would eventually equip 17 RAF squadrons.

An F.III, EE360, became the prototype Meteor F.IV and first flew in 1945, incorporating not just the lessons and experiences gained with the earlier Meteors, but two Derwent V engines as well. These each generated 3,500lbs thrust, significantly more than the 2400lbs (Derwent IV) of the F.III, and conferred a speed advantage at sea level of almost 100 mph for the F.IV (583mph) over the F.III (486mph). This increase in speed created its own set of problems when several early Meteor F.IV s broke up in flight during high-speed dives caused by excessive stresses within the structure of the wing. The solution was to reduce the span of the wing by 5ft 10in, resulting in a distinctive clipped wing appearance as well as enhancing the fighter's rate of roll. The F.IV operated with over 20 RAF squadrons, as well as numerous other units.

In June 1948, an official change occurred whereby Britain's air forces would cease to use Roman mark numbers; Arabic numerals would be used instead, thus Meteor F.IV for instance, became Meteor F.4.

For pilots converting to the new Meteor jet, the only 'dual' instruction available to the student was for him to sit in the aircraft cockpit with the instructor leaning over the student pilot's shoulder, pointing to certain levers, knobs and controls whilst uttering words of instruction. The student then took off!

Opposite top: Meteor F.3 EE419 bearing the markings MR-V of 245 Squadron which operated this mark during the period 1945 to 1948. This is an undated image, possibly taken at RAF Coltishall, Norfolk, showing EE419 finished in a pristine WW2/early post-war camouflage scheme, to which, at some point this aircraft had presumably been restored. It is included here as it is representative of the earlier Meteors; by the1960s, the period covered in this volume there were no F.3s and few if any F.4s still flying, excluding any surviving U.15s of course. (Ninety F.4s had been converted in the mid-1950s to become U.15 unmanned target aircraft).

Having served with 245 Squadron, EE419 went to the Central Flying School (CFS) at RAF Little Rissington, Gloucestershire, coded FDJ-G and later still to 206 Advanced Flying School (AFS) at RAF Oakington, Cambridgeshire, formed specifically to train Meteor pilots. By July 1960, EE419 had become 7247M as a gate guardian at Coltishall in natural metal finish. It was apparently burnt in 1969.

Opposite centre: Meteor T.7 WA721 at Coltishall on 14th August 1960. This T.7 is a little unusual in that it is equipped for target towing as indicated by the colour scheme applied to the underside. This variation was created by the emerging need in the 1950s for an effective target tug (TT) which could fly at speeds that better represented the speed range of the jet fighter and replace the Beaufighter, Tempest, Mosquito, Firefly and other piston-engined types then performing the TT role for both the RAF and FAA. By 1957, large numbers of Meteor T.7s and F.8s were surplus to requirements, consequently significant numbers of the latter were converted to become F(TT).8s, and a quantity of T.7s were also modified although they do not seem to have been officially designated T(TT).7s! Delivered in November 1950 WA721 served with 501, 23 and 74 Squadrons before being relegated to crash/rescue training duties in RAF Germany on 27th August 1963 and struck off charge.

Opposite bottom: Meteor T.7 WA671 at RAF Waddington, Lincolnshire, on 15th September 1962. Delivered in April 1950 WA671 was also converted to the TT role at some point judging by the black and yellow under surfaces, which has been over painted in part by the application of high visibility red in comparison with WA721 above. WA671 served with 600 and 608 Squadrons of the RAuxAF, Station Flights at RAF Linton-on-Ouse, Yorkshire, and RAF Middleton St.George, Durham, and then 111 and 74 Squadrons, before being struck off charge at RAF Wildenrath, West Germany in May 1964.

Above: Meteor T.7 WA721, RAF Coltishall on 13th August 1963, just two weeks before its demise in West Germany. A poorly lit image perhaps, but WA721 makes an interesting comparison with the photograph on page 9 taken almost exactly three years earlier.

Below: Meteor F.8 WK968 'C', in company with T.7 WL349 'Y', offer a comparison between the two marks. The date is not known but the location is believed to be RAF Manby. WK968 was operated by 64, 63, 56 and 46 Squadrons prior to being allocated to the RAFFC/RAFCAW coded 'A' later 'C'. Declared as a non-effective airframe in July 1969 this aircraft became a gate guardian at RAF Odiham, Hampshire, on 1st January 1970. WL349 never entered squadron service its flying time being spent with 229 OCU, ITS, CFE Communications Flight coded 'Y', 2 ANS and 1 ANS still coded 'Y', before returning to 229 OCU coded 'Z'. By 1976 WL349 had been sold into preservation.

Opposite page: Meteor T.7 WF791, Finningley, Yorkshire, on 14th September 1963. Delivered in March or April 1951, WF791 initially joined 26 Squadron before being allocated to a number of training units in succession, one of which was the Central Flying School (CFS) becoming number '27' as seen here, later it went on to serve with No.5 Civilian Anti-Aircraft Co-Operation Unit (CAACU) into the early 1970s. Ultimately WF791 was allocated a maintenance number which may not have been taken up but that would, ordinarily, have meant the end of its flying life: however, the Meteor was returned to flying status to become a part of the RAF's 'Vintage Pair' display team. Replaced in the team by WA669, WF791 was ultimately written off following a crash in May 1988. The distinctive marking on the nose is that of the CFS.

This system worked for hundreds of Meteor pilots in the first four years of the aircrafts operation, but was hardly ideal; a training variant was required and from that need emerged the Meteor T.7. Based on the short span F.4, the obvious differences between the two was the two-seat tandem cockpit arrangement enclosed by a heavily framed canopy, and lack of armament. The first production T.7 flew in October 1948, deliveries to the RAF commencing two months later.

As good as the F.4 was in its day, significant improvements were required in order for the Meteor to remain competitive. The successor to the F.4 was the Meteor F.8, immediately distinguished from its predecessor by virtue of an entirely new and enlarged tail unit, quite different in appearance and design to that of earlier Meteors and which improved the aircraft's general flying qualities. The F.8 also featured a longer fuselage (longer in fact than the two seat T.7), allowing an increase in internal fuel capacity, ejection seat, Derwent 8 engines and improved canopy amongst other refinements. Over 1000 F.8s were built with deliveries commencing in December 1949 to No1 Squadron. The F.8 remained Fighter Command's principal single seat fighter (supplemented by the Canadair Sabres of 66 and 92 Squadrons) until 1955 when, with the arrival of the Hawker Hunter into service, the F.8 began to fade from front line use.

The two final single seat Meteor designs to be produced (other than drone conversions) were both optimised for photographic reconnaissance, they were the FR.9 (Fighter Reconnaissance) and PR.10 (Photographic Reconnaissance). The FR.9, was in essence an F.8 featuring a new nose design that incorporated three glass panels for the cameras accommodated within, enabling the FR.9 to conduct its principal role of low-level tactical reconnaissance. It entered service with No.2 Squadron in December 1950. The four nose-mounted 20mm cannon carried by all of the Meteor single seat fighter variants, were retained in the FR.9. The PR.10 was an unarmed high-altitude strategic reconnaissance aircraft, featuring the tail section and long span wing of the early F.4 and FR.9 nose. Deliveries also commenced in December 1950.

The last four Meteor variants were all night fighters (NF) designed and built by Armstrong Whitworth Aircraft, as the Gloster company was stretched to capacity with single seat Meteor production. They became the NF.11, NF.12, NF.13 and NF.14. Principally, these aircraft all featured a much extended fuselage – the nose of which accommodated the radar equipment. Other features included a tandem cockpit, F.8 style tail plane and relocation of the four cannon to the aircrafts wings, displaced of course by the radar. The first production NF.11, WD585, flew in October 1950 with deliveries to the RAF commencing the following August, replacing the De Havilland Mosquitoes of 29 Squadron. The NF.12, introduced to service from April 1953, featured American designed radar of superior

performance to that installed in the NF.11, in consequence the NF.12 required a longer nose, which in turn required a distinctively modified tail of increased area to compensate. The NF.13 was in essence an NF.11 modified for service in tropical areas, deliveries commencing in January 1953. The last mark, the NF.14 was also the last of any Meteor variant to remain in front-line operational service with an RAF squadron; as distinct from those Meteors allocated to operational squadrons equipped with later types e.g. 29 Squadron; equipped with Javelins but with a few Meteors still attached. The honour of the last operational flight belonged to WS787 of No.60 Squadron and occurred on 17th August 1961 at Seletar, Singapore. The NF.14 was essentially an NF.12 that introduced the clear-vision sliding canopy – replacing the T.7 style canopy of the three earlier NF marks and, ejection seats. Deliveries commenced from November 1953. Following their withdrawal from front-line duties, some NF.14s were converted to become NF(T).14s by replacing their radar with additional radio equipment. This version of the Meteor saw service with the Advanced Navigation Schools.

The U.15 (Unmanned) was an F.4 converted to a drone; an unmanned radio controlled target aircraft, which could still be flown manually, from the cockpit if required. The prototype U.15 flew in March 1955, the first of ninety conversions. U.16 later D.16 (Drone) referred to the F.8 drone conversion. The Meteor mark numbers 17, 18 and 19 were not used. TT.20 was a target-tug conversion of the NF.11, which became available for these duties with the arrival of the NF.14 into service, displacing the NF.11 as it did so. Fifty were modified from 1956, the type remaining in service until 1970.

Top: Meteor T.7 VW452 at RAF Waddington on 19th September 1964. The first RAF unit to receive VW452 was the Central Fighter Establishment (CFE) before passing onto 613 and then 43 Squadrons, followed by a period at the Royal Air Force Flying College (RAFFC), Manby, Lincolnshire. On 1st July 1962 the RAFFC disbanded at Manby becoming the Royal Air Force College of Air Warfare (RAF-CAW) on the same day at the same location. VW452 was retained by the new unit receiving the individual code letter 'S', as seen in this image and, as far as is known, remained there for the rest of its flying life, ultimately being recorded on the dump at RAF Catterick, Yorkshire in July 1972.

Above: Meteor T.7 WL378, coded 'W', date and location unknown. This aircraft operated with a number of units including in turn, 16 and 612 Squadrons, 228

Operational Conversion Unit (OCU), 25, 46, 25 (i.e. twice), 64 and 85 Squadrons, 229 OCU and 85 Squadron once more. The latter squadron had operated Meteor night fighter variants (NF.11, NF.12 and NF.14) from 1951 to 1958 and would have possessed T.7s for training purposes, until re-equipped with the Gloster Javelin in late 1958. On 31st March 1963 85 Squadron disbanded but reformed the next day when the Fighter Command Target Facilities Squadron at West Raynham, Norfolk, became 85 Squadron equipped with Canberra B.2, T.4, T.11, Meteor F.8s and the ubiquitous T.7. WL378 is devoid of any squadron markings but it is known that the individual letter code 'W' was applied when operated by 85 Squadron for the second time, so presumably this Meteor is seen between April 1963 and August 1972, by which date it was at Catterick to be burnt whilst training firemen in their vital role.

Top: Meteor T.7 WA714, date, location and unit unknown. Delivered on 10th October 1950, this aircraft was first operated by 205 AFS at Middleton St.George, which had formed the previous month to train day-fighter pilots on Meteors with a complement of 17 T.7s (plus 17 F.4s and possibly a few F.3s). This aircraft went on to serve with the CFS, 71 Squadron, RAF Wildenrath Station Flight and the Royal Aircraft Establishment (RAE) at Farnborough, prior to being struck off charge in September 1968.

Above: Meteor T.7 WH208 coded '70', Swinderby, Lincolnshire, mid-1962. Delivered on 7th February 1952 WH208 served with 612 and 611 Squadrons, of the Royal Auxiliary Air Force, later returning to 612 before moving to the Bomber Command Communication Squadron (BCCS), this was followed by a move to No.5 Flying Training School (FTS) at RAF Oakington. The next unit to receive WH208 was 8 FTS, then the RAFCAW, and finally 229 OCU. This aircraft was damaged whilst landing at Bovingdon on 23rd June 1967 and struck off charge three weeks later. Whilst serving with 8 FTS, WH208 had been allocated the individual number '70', so presumably this image shows the aircraft during its time with 8 FTS which had reformed at Driffield on 1st June 1954, moved to Swinderby in 1955, where this photograph was taken, finally disbanding there (permanently this time), on 19th March 1964.

Top: It is cheating; Meteor T.7 G-ANSO did not enter British military service, but colour images of this aircraft are rare, therefore it ought not to be excluded. G-ANSO, previously Gloster's private venture ground attack aircraft 'Reaper', was a modified Meteor F.8 that was later converted to receive a T.7 nose and cockpit in place of the original. The F.8's tail unit was retained; producing a variant sometimes termed the T.7½, never an official designation, but it made its point! The aircraft was sold to Sweden in 1958, acquiring the civil registration SE-DCC, for use as a target tug, following which it was preserved in Sweden. This image was taken in September 1954 at Farnborough when the aircraft was painted 'larkspur blue'.

Above: An unidentified Meteor F.8 coded 'S' of 615 Squadron, location unknown, displaying the Squadron's markings on either side of the fuselage roundel as well as its tail. This unit was a Royal Auxiliary Air Force squadron, so the photograph had to have been taken before 10th March 1957, the date on which the Royal Auxiliary Air Force was disbanded. A very brief note attached to this image states that it was the Commanding Officer's aircraft; perhaps explaining the colourful tail which lacks the individual code letter commonly applied to the F.8s operated by 615 Squadron. There is a very strong possibility that this is WH445 which did carry the individual code 'S' and the tail markings shown here, if so, its code letter was later changed to 'B' at an unknown date, thus setting the date of this photograph back further still. WH445 was sold as scrap in May 1958 having only ever served with 615 Squadron.

Top: Meteor F.8 7354M ex WE859 seen at RAF Halton, Buckinghamshire, during 1958 or 1959. WE859 was delivered to the RAF on the 3rd May 1951 and entered service with 41 Squadron, later moving to 600 Squadron where it wore the individual code 'P'. By 20th June 1956, WE859 had been allocated to No. 1 School of Technical Training at Halton, with the maintenance serial 7354M as seen here whilst retaining its 600 Squadron colours on the fuselage. 7354M was eventually scrapped. To the left is another ex 600 Squadron F.8 that could conceivably be 7294M, previously WF759.

Above: Meteor F.8 VZ473, 29th October 1962, at Stansted Fire School. Listed by all sources as an F.8, VZ473 had been fitted with an FR.9 (Fighter-Reconnaissance) type nose at some point in a career that seems to have been restricted to time spent with the A&AEE, Boscombe Down, Wiltshire, as a Ministry of Supply (MoS) operated aircraft. (The MoS had absorbed the earlier Ministry of Aircraft Production and its responsibilities in April 1946). VZ473 arrived at Boscombe Down on 25th April 1950 and is known to have been involved in flying and firing trials utilising various combinations of rocket projectile installations, beyond which little seems to have been recorded! Looking somewhat desolate and remote in this location, the aircraft would appear to be in a very good external condition.

Above: Meteor F.8 WK968 believed to be at RAF Manby in company with other Meteors belonging to the RAFFC/RAFCAW. This aircraft's details are related on page 10. Aircraft 'A' and 'B' beyond are presumably two of the three seen in flight on the title page.

Below: Meteor F.8 'WH456' coded 'L', resplendent in 616 Squadron colours, RAF Finningley, September 1969. WH456 had operated with 616 Squadron before being sold for scrap in May 1958. The presence of the camouflaged Vulcan B.2 XH554 (delivered in April 1961) indicates that this is much later than 1957/58. This Meteor's true identity is WL168, it had been delivered to

the RAF in early 1954 prior to being issued to 111 Squadron in April that year and to 604 Squadron in July 1955, before joining the APS at RAF Sylt in January 1959 as an F(TT).8. In September 1961, WL168 was flown back to the UK and placed in storage at RAF Lynham. Struck off charge in April 1962 became 7750M the following month and, later, transferred to RAF Finningley. Presumably, it was whilst at Finningley that the Meteor was painted to represent WH456 of 616 Squadron, the unit having been based there between May 1946 and May 1955, before moving to Worksop, Nottinghamshire. This aircraft now resides with the Yorkshire Air Museum, painted to represent WK864, itself an ex 616 Squadron aircraft that was scrapped in 1963.

Top: Meteor F.8 VZ508, 5 CAACU RAF Woodvale, Lancashire, 17th May 1971. This aircraft first served with the Air Fighting Development Squadron; a unit within the CFE, followed by service with 43 and 151 Squadrons until late 1955. Having left squadron service, VZ508 was allocated to the Temperature and Humidity Flight (THUM), a unit formed on 1st May 1951 at RAF Hooton Park, Wirral, moving soon after to Woodvale. The THUM's duty was to obtain meteorological information from altitudes commencing at 1,500 ft at regular intervals up to 30,000+ft daily, and has become famous retrospectively for being the last RAF unit to utilise the Supermarine Spitfire in an operational capacity, most notably PR.19s (PR.XIX originally), which remained in use until as late as June 1957! Mosquitoes replaced the Spitfires, jets were not then considered suitable for the role of collecting such data, so precisely what the Meteor's role within THUM was is unclear; perhaps they were used for trials to establish their level of suitability.

On 1st January 1958, THUM Flight and VZ508 were absorbed into 5 CAACU that had relocated to Woodvale on the same day, and remained with the unit for over 14 years. In early 1972 the aircraft was dispatched for conversion to a U.16, (later D.16), on completion VZ508 was ultimately allocated to RAE Llanbedr, Merioneth, and presumably expired there!

Above: Meteor F.8 WH453, 5 CAACU Woodvale, 5th May 1971. Delivered into squadron service in March 1952, this aircraft operated with 222 and 72 Squadrons prior to being delivered to 5 CAACU in May 1956, remaining with the unit until October 1971. Following a period in storage WH453 was sent for conversion to become a U.16/D.16 drone in April 1972 and, as with the case of VZ508, ultimately served at Llanbedr. In the autumn of 1990, WH453 was grounded, eventually being acquired in 2005 by the Bentwaters Cold War Museum, Suffolk, where it is to revert to its original mark.

Top: Strictly speaking outside of the period of this title, but added for the sake of comparison. Meteor D.16 WH453 coded 'L', 10th June 1990, Boscombe Down, having flown in from RAE Llanbedr two days previously. At that time, it was one of only two operational Meteor drones left in service, both operated by the Defence Research Agency at Llanbedr. Apart from the colour scheme, the extended nose was perhaps the most obvious difference between the F.8 and D.16. *Author's collection*

Below: Meteor NF.14 WS810, date and location unknown. Shown wearing the colours of 264 Squadron on the fuselage, this image must have been taken between October 1954 and 30th September 1957, the period during which this mark was operated by 264 Squadron and on which latter date the squadron disbanded. It has been suggested that the nose radome may also be indicative of

a date, as it is not yet painted black! WS810 was delivered in March 1954 and, as stated, served with 264 Squadron coded 'B', later 'V', before transferring to 33 Squadron that reformed on 30th September 1957 at RAF Leeming, Yorkshire, by renumbering 264 Squadron. The Meteors of 33 Squadron were replaced in July 1958 by the Gloster Javelin, the displaced aircraft being allocated elsewhere or struck off charge. WS810 however, was sent to the Far East to join 60 Squadron at RAF Tengah, Singapore, which assumed an all-weather role in October 1959 following the adoption of the Meteor NF.14. This squadron would prove to be the last front-line unit to use the Meteor in operational service with the RAF, retaining NF.14s until replaced by the Javelin from mid-1961. For the record NF.14 WS787 made the last operational flight of an RAF Meteor, on 17th August 1961. WS810 was struck off charge on 8th September 1961 at RAF Seletar, Singapore.

Top: Meteor F.8 WH291 'T', date and location unknown, but possibly at RAF Binbrook, Lincolnshire, displays 85 Squadron colours on the fuselage and wingtips as well as the squadron's distinctive hexagonal marking on the fin. WH291 was delivered to the RAF on 19th November 1951 and first issued to 257 Squadron that operated the F.8 until the winter of 1954/55 when the Meteor was relinquished to be replaced by the Hunter. Displaced from 257 Squadron, WH291 went to the RAFFC/RAFCAW with whom it remained until passed to 85 Squadron which reformed in April 1963, equipped with Meteor F.8s amongst other marks and types for its target facilities role (see T.7 WL378 on page 12). Later still, this aircraft was allocated to 229 OCU with which it ended its service flying days and by August 1974 was stored at No.5 Maintenance Unit, RAF Kemble, Gloucestershire, before being sold into preservation on 10th February 1976.

Above: Meteor F.8 WK786 'P', RAF Coltishall 13th August 1963. Delivered on 21st August 1952, this aircraft was first allocated to 72 Squadron and wore the individual code 'T'. This was followed by service with the Armament Practice Station (APS) RAF Sylt, West Germany, where the individual code 'P' was allocated. Diagonal black and yellow TT markings are visible on the undersides that indicates WK786 had become an F(TT).8 at some point in its life. By 3rd August 1962, the aircraft had returned to the UK and was reported to be on the dump at RAF Coltishall; however, if the date shown here is correct, it would appear that this Meteor survived on display for some time, albeit in a gradually deteriorating condition.

Top: Meteor NF.14 WS777, RAF Coltishall, 5th July 1959. Delivered in February 1954 and later allocated to 85 Squadron, which operated the mark from April 1954 until 31st October 1958 when 85 Squadron disbanded. When this image was taken, WS777 was operated by 12 Group Communication Flight, based then at RAF Newton, Nottinghamshire, although relocation to RAF Horsham St. Faith was completed the following month. The unit remained there until 31st March 1963 on which date it disbanded, its aircraft being allocated elsewhere. It would appear that WS777 was not flown again, having been allocated

the maintenance serial 7813M in June 1963, followed by a move to RAF Buchan in Scotland, to serve as a gate guardian, before perishing on the fire dump at RAF Leuchars, Fife, from 1974.

Above: Meteor TT.20 WD679 'T', 3/4 CAACU, Exeter, July 1964. Delivered in February 1952 as an NF.11, WD679 was operated by 87 Squadron prior to conversion to TT.20 and service at Exeter. This aircraft was written off there on 16th July 1968 following an overshoot. It was sold as scrap the following May.

Top: Meteor TT.20 WM224 'X', 3/4 CAACU, Exeter, Devon, July 1964. Delivered as an NF.11 WM224 served with 228 OCU and 29 Squadron prior to conversion to a target tug. As a TT.20 this aircraft operated with 3/4 CAACU before transferring to 5 CAACU, after which it had become 8177M at RAF Swanton Morley, Norfolk, by October 1971. Bought for preservation, WM224 now resides at the East Midlands Airport Aeropark.

Above: Meteor TT.20 WD630 'Q' 3/4 CAACU Exeter, July 1964. A poorly lit image which nevertheless provides a view of the starboard wing-mounted winch.

Delivered in October 1951 as an NF.11, this aircraft operated in turn with 151, 125 and 5 Squadrons, following which it was converted to TT.20 configuration and assigned to 3/4 CAACU for target towing duties. This unit had resulted from the merger on 1st July 1954 of 3 CAACU, based at Exeter and 4 CAACU at Llandow, Glamorgan. The new unit remained located at Exeter until disbanding on the last day of 1971. On 1st May 1970, 7 Squadron reformed at St.Mawgan, Cornwall, with the Canberra TT.18 in the target facilities role, later assuming the duties of 3/4 CAACU. As for WD630, it was apparently sold as scrap in March 1975.

Top: Meteor NF.14 WS845 '6' 'Empire Test Pilots School' on forward fuselage, Stansted Fire School, 29th October 1962. Delivered in May 1954 this aircraft had spent time with Rolls-Royce at Hucknall, Nottinghamshire, before joining 64 and 72 Squadrons. This was followed in turn by allocation to the Empire Test Pilots School (ETPS), located at Farnborough, Hampshire, in those days attached to the RAE. The individual code '6' was allocated whilst with the ETPS. WS845 was struck off charge in February 1962 and delivered to Stansted to perish.

Above: Meteor NF.12 WD687 Stansted Fire School, 29th October 1962. Delivered in July 1952, this aircraft had been built as an NF.11, retained by the MoS, becoming the second prototype NF.12 for the latter's development programme. On 28th January 1953, WD687 arrived at the A&AEE and commenced trials of a new fin design required to compensate for the longer forward fuselage of the NF.12. The 'scalloped' appearance of the new fin was distinctively different to that of the NF.11 and NF.13 and increased the overall area by approximately one square foot, producing the required result. Little else seems to be recorded for WD687, other than its arrival at Stansted and its ultimate demise there!

Top: Meteor NF.12 marked as 7065M, 26th December 1969. This aircraft had originally been delivered in September 1953 as NF.12 WS692 and served with 46 and 72 Squadrons bearing the individual code 'C' with both units. The faded squadron colours either side of the fuselage roundel are those of 72 Squadron which had relinquished its final NF.12s in mid 1959, replacing them with the Javelin. Following its squadron service, WS692 became 7605M at the RAF Technical College, Henlow, Bedfordshire, in July 1959; however, the maintenance number was incorrectly applied as 7065M, (actually allocated to Vampire F.1, TG312). On 31st December 1965, the RAF Technical College disbanded and its duties merged with those of the RAF College, Cranwell, Lincolnshire. This aircraft was subsequently preserved and now resides with the Newark Air Museum.

Above: Somewhat off the beaten path, but a Meteor none-the-less, is this Swedish civil registered TT.20, SE-DCF. Originally one of 20 NF.11s ordered for the Royal Danish Air Force (RDAF), it was one of six later converted to the TT role by Armstrong Whitworth, at its Bitterswell facility in Leicestershire. SE-DCF had previously been coded 512 with RDAF, and was one of four subsequently sold on to Sweden. It is seen here prior to delivery to its new owner. The wing-mounted winch is very evident.

Vickers Valiant

The Vickers Valiant was the first of the 'V' bomber trilogy to enter RAF service, equipping 232 OCU and later, 138 Squadron at RAF Gaydon, Warwickshire, receiving its first Valiants from February 1955.

The prototype Vickers Valiant, WB210 first flew on 18th May 1951, but was destroyed the following January following an in-flight fire. Its duties were subsequently undertaken by the second prototype WB215, which first flew in April 1952. Vickers received an initial order for 25 Valiant B.1s (including five pre-production aircraft) in April 1951, the first of which, pre-production airframe WP199, flew in December 1953.

Designed as a fast, high level heavy bomber, the Valiant, combined with the Canberra light bomber, represented a quantum leap in capability for the RAF, especially when compared to the piston-engined 'heavies' i.e. the Boeing Washington, (retired in 1954) and Avro Lincoln, that still served Bomber Command as a heavy bomber in 1955.

The Valiant was operated by 232 OCU, numbers 7, 18, 49, 90, 138, 148, 199, 207, 214, and 543 Squadrons – this latter unit becoming a dedicated strategic reconnaissance squadron. The last Valiant delivered was XD875 in August 1957, at which point two prototypes and 104 production Valiants had been completed. Several more were cancelled, as was the Valiant B.2, of which only one example flew.

The high altitudes, at which the world's bombers sought to operate in the 1950s, had become an increasingly hostile environment by 1960/61, with the advent of credible ground-to-air and air-to-air anti-aircraft missile systems. It became necessary therefore to fly at low level in order to penetrate enemy territory and avoid radar detection. The Valiant was no exception, and the transition from high to low level began in the early 1960s, even though it was known that by operating the Valiant at low level for extended periods, an environment for which it was not designed, excessive stresses would be created that would weaken the airframe; there was however little choice in the matter! This period of change, from high to low operating altitudes was marked in a sense by the later application of a green, grey and white camouflage scheme that replaced the earlier overall anti-flash white. Despite a reduction in individual aircraft flying time, cracks were discovered in the wing spars of the Valiant force and the decision was made to retire the remaining fleet of approximately 60 surviving aircraft. By January 1965, the last Valiant had been withdrawn. This decision incidentally, caused the immediate loss to the RAF of its fleet of aerial tankers, a role in which

Valiant-equipped No 214 Squadron had been operating for several years and No 90 Squadron since 1961; both units becoming dedicated to that single role in early 1962, thus losing their alternative bombing commitment.

Valiants did go to war briefly, participating in the Suez conflict in late 1956. They were also involved in the extensive testing of Britain's nuclear bombs, dropping both atomic and hydrogen bombs in 1956 and 1957 respectively.

The Valiant carried a crew of five and was equipped to carry either nuclear weapons or a conventional bomb load of up to 21,000lbs. In common with the other 'V' bombers, no defensive armament was carried. The B.1 had a wingspan of 114ft 4in, was 108ft 3in in length and could achieve a speed of 567mph at 30,000ft; power being supplied by four Rolls-Royce Avon 204 turbojets of 10,050 lbs thrust each, buried within the inner wing in individual bays. The internal fuel capacity of approximately 6,700 gallons could be enhanced, when required, by utilising two external tanks mounted beneath the wings, each with a capacity of 1,645 gallons. The service ceiling was approximately 54,000 ft.

Opposite: Valiant BK.1 XD820, RAF Waddington 19th September 1964. Delivered in October 1956, this Valiant served with 148, 90 and 214 Squadrons before returning to 90 Squadron once more, which, as stated was one of the RAF's two dedicated AAR units. This series of images was taken at almost the very end of the Valiant's service and show the aircraft resplendent in its recently applied camouflage finish, which until mid-1964 was still wearing its earlier overall white scheme. XD820 was broken up at RAF Honington, Suffolk, in February 1965.

Opposite page: Three views of Valiant B(PR)K.1 WZ393, RAF Waddington 14th September 1962, a day or so prior to Waddington's Battle of Britain air show. First flown on 9th March 1956 and delivered the following month, WZ393 operated with 214, 90 and 148 Squadrons prior to being struck off charge and scrapped at RAF Marham, Norfolk, in March 1965. In these views, the size and scale of the auxiliary fuel tanks and pylons are clearly evident.

Top: Valiants B(PR)K.1 WZ390 with BK.1 XD812 leading, both from 214 Squadron, Marham, practising air-to-air (AAR) refuelling on 7th January 1962. This squadron had been tasked with the development of AAR in December 1957, and to test the Valiant's suitability in that role. Suitable modifications to the aircraft were required of course including such essentials as the installation of additional fuel tanks in the bomb bay, a hose and drum unit delivery system and nose mounted refuelling probe, amongst other items. The trials of systems, aircraft and techniques, were ultimately successful and approval was obtained in April 1959 for the RAF to establish a force of 16 Valiant tankers. WZ390 seen here, established an RAF record in May 1960 by flying non-stop from Marham to Singapore using AAR. In 1961, approval was granted for 90 Squadron to become

the second tanker squadron in the RAF and conversion to the role began. The two units would prove to be the only ones to use the Valiant for AAR. Interestingly these two units maintained a dual role, retaining their bombing function, nominally at least, until they were released from the latter in 1962! WZ390 was scrapped at Marham in early 1965, whilst apparently XD812 went to Shoeburyness on Foulness Island, Essex, in 1965. It is possible that XD812 was used to test the effect of various types of munitions on the airframe. Nowadays the facility is known as the Defence Science & Technology Laboratory.

Above: Valiant B(PR).1 WZ382, RAF Waddington 15th September 1962. First flown in January 1955 WZ382 seems only to have been operated by one unit, namely 543 Squadron, a dedicated strategic reconnaissance unit. This squadron had reformed in April, June, July or September 1955, (sources conflict!) at RAF Gaydon, receiving the Valiant shortly afterwards. Only the second squadron to receive the aircraft, it is perhaps indicative of the critical importance attached to aerial reconnaissance. After being withdrawn from flying duties WZ382 was allocated the maintenance serial 7873M. Scrapping occurred at RAF Wyton, Huntingdonshire, in 1965.

Above and below: Valiant BK.1 XD816, bearing 214 Squadron's motif on the tail. The location and date is unknown although faint pencil marks on the image's frame states '1968', which of course ought to be impossible given that the remaining Valiant fleet was scrapped in 1965. However, this aircraft had been maintained in an airworthy condition in order to conduct fatigue trials with the British Aircraft Corporation (BAC) to whom it had been transferred in mid-1964. The trials continued until early 1968, after which XD816 was flown to Abingdon prior to 1st April 1968 to participate in the RAF's 50th Anniversary celebration, presumably on static display. The Valiant subsequently remained at Abingdon until August 1970, when it was scrapped – with only the cockpit section surviving. XD816 had been delivered in September 1956 and later served with 148 and 214 Squadrons and, of course, has the distinction of being the last Valiant to fly.

Above: Valiant BK.1 XD872, Waddington, 14th September 1963. Delivered in June 1957 XD872 was retained for a short time by the manufacturer before moving to the A&AEE on 8th July 1957 for various trials which included a period at Idris in Libya. Following its service with the A&AEE XD872 served with 138 Squadron, BCDU, 7 and 90 Squadrons, finally being scrapped at RAF Wyton in June 1965. When this image was taken, XD872 was operated by 90 Squadron in the air-to-air refuelling (AAR) role.

Below: Valiant B(PR) K.1 WZ397, date and location not known. First flown in April 1956 and delivered the following June this aircraft appears only to have served with 214 and 543 Squadrons before being struck off charge in March 1965, at which point it became 7888M before being scrapped later that year.

Opposite page: Two further views of XD820. See caption on page 25.

Above: Valiant BK.1 XD857, Hucknall, 12th May 1964. Delivered in January 1957, this aircraft appears only to have served with 49 Squadron which retained the type until the end of 1964. XD857 was struck off charge in March 1965 and scrapped, although, as with XD816, the cockpit section was preserved.

Below: Valiant BK.1 XD818. Seen at RAF Marham in the early years following retirement and retained as a guardian at its Norfolk base. XD818 was delivered in September 1956 and allocated to 49 Squadron two months later. It was this aircraft that released Britain's prototype hydrogen bomb on 15th May 1957, the aircraft being piloted by the Squadron's commanding officer, the late Wing Commander (later Group Captain), Ken Hubbard, DFC, OBE, AFC. XD818 survived (as a complete airframe) into preservation, to be later transferred to the RAF Museum Hendon, where it remained for many years displayed in its original overall white colour scheme. More recently, XD818 has been moved to the RAF Museum at Cosford, Shropshire, as part of the National Cold War Exhibition.

Blackburn Beverley

The RAF appropriately named it after the cathedral town of Beverley in the East Riding of Yorkshire ...

The Blackburn Beverley originated from a design produced by General Aircraft Ltd (GAL) which, during world war two, had produced the Hamilcar glider; a particularly large aircraft, featuring a wingspan of 110ft, a deep fuselage and the ability to carry a light tank. General Aircraft later experimented with a variant of the Hamilcar glider powered by two Bristol Mercury engines, following which, the company began to consider ideas for a larger transport aircraft powered by four engines. Whilst pursuing their design concepts, the Air Ministry issued Specification C3/46 that required an aircraft capable of performing duties which included supply-dropping, troop-carrying, parachuting and casualty evacuation plus, the ability to operate from rough airstrips. General Aircraft tendered and was rewarded with a contract for one aircraft designated GAL60 and later termed the Universal Freighter Mark 1 in a (unsuccessful) bid to attract civil interest. The new aircraft was powered by four Bristol Hercules engines fitted with four bladed propellers on a shoulder-mounted wing, a fixed tricycle undercarriage and was unpressurised. The GAL60 was of very similar appearance to the later Beverley, its most obvious external difference, at first, being the two 6ft 6in diameter main wheels, which were later replaced by a Beverley-style undercarriage. In 1949, the GAL60 was transported by road from General Aircraft's premises to the Blackburn Aircraft Ltd factory at Brough; General Aircraft having merged with Blackburn earlier that year. Following reassembly and roll out, the aircraft flew for the first time on 20th June 1950, painted in RAF livery and markings and allocated the serial WF320. Flight-testing was very successful, and the aircraft was passed to the A&AEE for trials which were also deemed to have been successfully completed.

Because of the GAL60's success, a second prototype, the GAL65, (designated by Blackburn as type B-100) Universal Freighter Mark 2 was ordered in September 1950 by the Ministry of Supply (MoS), the construction of which commenced in 1952 and was first flown in June 1953 as WZ889. The GAL65 was an extensive redesign of its predecessor incorporating many changes and improvements, the most obvious external changes included a redesigned tail boom to accommodate up to 36 passengers, a modified fuselage fitted with clamshell doors and Bristol Centaurus engines.

Although civil operators showed a complete lack of interest in the Universal Freighter, the MoS did, and an initial order was placed in late 1952 for 20 aircraft. The RAF appropriately named it after the cathedral town of Beverley, in the East Riding of Yorkshire in which Brough is located. The aircraft became the Beverley C.1 in service use. Later orders increased the total RAF procurement to 47 aircraft. The production aircraft, designated B-101 by the manufacturer, incorporated several minor changes over the preceding GAL65, but in most respects the two aircraft were very similar.

XB259 and XB260 were the first to fly on 29th January 1955, and 30th March 1955 respectively, although they were not the first to enter squadron service, as they were retained by the manufacturer for a series of trials. The following two, XB261 and XB262, were sent to the A&AEE at Boscombe Down, whilst XB263 was allocated to the RAF Handling Squadron also located at Boscombe Down, in December 1955. XB265 was the first Beverley to enter squadron service, joining RAF Abingdon-based 47 Squadron, coded 'A' on 12th March 1956, beating XB264 'C' to the same unit by one week! (For the record, 'B' was XB267, which joined the unit on 14th March). The second unit to receive the new aircraft was 53 Squadron which moved to Abingdon, Oxfordshire, and began training with the Beverley from January (or February – sources conflict!) 1957, with the help of 47 Squadron crews, during the course of which XH117 was lost in a fatal crash on 5th March 1957 near Abingdon. By early April 1957, the squadron was operational and, together with 47 Squadron, the two units operated as a Wing until June 1963, when the squadrons merged to create a much larger 47 Squadron consisting of four flights rather than two. The Beverley was retained by the Squadron, at Abingdon until 31st October 1967, on which date the unit disbanded, reforming in February 1968, at RAF Fairford, Gloucestershire, equipped with the Lockheed C-130 Hercules. In the meantime 53 Squadron reformed in late 1965, prior to receiving the Short Belfast C.1 in January 1966.

Opposite: **Beverley XL131 at RAF Finningley in September 1965. See caption on contents page.**

No. 30 Squadron was the next to equip with the Beverley, commencing in April 1957, at RAF Dishforth, Yorkshire, where it remained until November 1959 when it moved to RAF Eastleigh, in Kenya, remaining there until moving to RAF Muharraq, Bahrain in September 1964. No.30 Squadron was disbanded at Muharraq on 6th September 1967, and as with 47 Squadron, the unit reformed and equipped with the Hercules, in 1968.

No.84 Squadron based at RAF Khormaksar, Aden, a squadron, which, incidentally, has never been based in the United Kingdom, re-equipped with the Beverley commencing in late May and early June 1958 and quickly attained its operational strength of six aircraft. Concentrating primarily on tactical support for the ground forces employed in the troubled hot spot that Aden once was, 84 Squadron remained at Khormaksar until 1967. In August or September 1967 (sources conflict!), the Squadron moved to Sharjah, Oman, but the Beverleys didn't; they were flown back to the UK for eventual disposal, (the last three examples having left Aden by early November), whilst 84 Squadron re-equipped at Sharjah with the Hawker Siddeley Andover.

The final Beverley squadron to form was 34 Squadron, which reformed on 1st October 1960 at Seletar, Singapore. This unit acquired four Beverleys from 48 Squadron based at RAF Changi, Singapore, the latter unit being the RAF's resident Far East transport squadron during the 1950s and early/mid 1960s. Although it is well known that 48 Squadron operated the Douglas Dakota, Vickers Valetta and Handley Page Hastings transport aircraft during that period, the allocation of four Beverleys is less well documented. They had been received in 1959 to test both the aircraft's suitability to a tropical climate and to provide a medium range heavy lift capability that the RAF's Far East Air Force then lacked; they acquitted themselves well. The four examples that comprised the 48 Squadron Beverley Flight were XB260, XB262, XM104 and XM112. XM104 joined first, on 13th February 1959, followed at intervals by XB260 in April, XM112 in May and XB262 on 5th June 1959. As stated 34 Squadron reformed in 1960 using these four Beverleys as their nucleus until December 1960 when XM120 arrived. Very gradually after that, a further six aircraft were allocated, the eleventh and last, XL150 being received in March 1966. On 31st December 1967, 34 Squadron disbanded and has not reformed since.

Mention should be made of 242 Operational Conversion Unit based at RAF Dishforth, Yorkshire, and later, RAF Thorney Island, Sussex. This unit had

Above: **Beverley XL131 at Finningley in September 1965. See caption on contents page.**

formed on 16th April 1951 to convert aircrews to operate various types of transport aircraft with which the RAF was equipped. From 1957, a Beverley Flight was formed within the OCU. Generally operating two or three such aircraft at any one time, the Flight trained almost 200 Beverley aircrews before disbanding in March 1967.

During the Beverley's relatively short service career of just under 12 years, the aircraft was subject to relatively few modifications, the principle 'mod' being the introduction of improved Centaurus engines as referred to in the technical description, although, to the casual observer, the change was less than obvious. A far more obvious change to the Beverley was the introduction of a camouflage scheme for those aircraft operating in the Middle East. From late 1964, several Beverleys were flown to 32 MU, RAF St.Athan in Wales to receive a camouflage scheme of Dark Earth and Mid-Stone with Anti-Searchlight Gloss Black under surfaces, although there was a concession to the Beverley's crew whereby the flight-deck roof remained white in order to reflect the sun's heat. The original intention had been to camouflage all of the aircraft, but the heat from the sun made overseas operations intolerable for the crews, so a portion of the Beverleys original colour scheme was retained.

Immediately following its entry into service, the Beverley was worked hard flying supplies to British Forces and on disaster relief missions around the world, often operating in difficult 'hot and high' conditions. Although possessing an impressive load carrying capability and very good short field performance the Beverley was slow, additionally, when a full load was carried, the aircraft was lacking in range. It was perhaps inevitable then that as Britain progressively withdrew from Empire, faster and longer-ranged aircraft would be needed which did not require the use of numerous intermediate staging posts.

The arrival of the Lockheed Hercules caused a rapid phase-out of the Beverley from early 1967 in the UK, with many aircraft being flown directly to 27 Maintenance Unit at RAF Shawbury, Shropshire, or 71 MU, RAF Bicester, Oxfordshire, for scrapping – although two (XB269 and XB290) are known to have made a formation flypast over Upavon, Wiltshire on 7th December 1967, before continuing their final flight to 27 MU. The last squadron aircraft were withdrawn in December 1967 when 34 Squadron disbanded and its aircraft scrapped in Singapore, although one or two of their aircraft are known to have been flown in early January 1968.

At least two Beverleys continued to fly for a time following withdrawal of the remainder of the fleet; XB261 made its final flight on 6th October 1971, when it was flown to Southend for preservation from Boscombe Down, the A&AEE having been the only unit with which this aircraft had ever served. XB261 was scrapped in May 1983. XB259 was, as stated above, the first Beverley to fly and spent the majority of its time with the RAE at Farnborough until it was retired at the end of 1972. Bought by Court Line, a civilian operator and intended to be used to transport aircraft engines and heavy equipment around Europe, it would seem that, due to financial difficulties, XB259 was never used. Consequently, the aircraft was sold once again and on 30th March 1974, it was flown for the last time – the last ever flight of any Beverley – into preservation with the Museum of Army Transport at Beverley, where it remained until transferred by road on 23rd May 2004 to Fort Paull near Hull. It was reassembled and reopened to the public on 30th April 2005. As of late 2007, XB259 remains the only complete Beverley extant – currently residing at Fort Paull.

The Beverley's basic technical description was as follows:

Crew	Four		Recommended cruising speed	173mph at 12,500 ft
Wing Span	162ft		Maximum altitude	16,000ft.
Length	99ft 5in		Range without payload	3,710 miles
Height	38ft 9in			
Weight empty	79,200lb		Range with 29,000lb payload	1,300 miles
Maximum weight	135,000lb, (increased by 7,000lbs in emergencies)		Range with 44,000lb payload	200 miles
Maximum speed	238mph at 5,700ft,			

Engines
Four Bristol Centaurus 173 or (later) 175, 18 cylinder radial engines. The Centaurus 173 was replaced by the 175 following a series of sudden engine failures from May 1962, caused by faulty cylinder holding down bolts shearing, which could, in turn, cause a cylinder to disintegrate and catch fire. An engine replacement programme was subsequently initiated. Both the 173 and 175 delivered 2,675 hp each, increased to 2,850hp when water/methanol injection was employed at take-off. Each engine was provided with a 10-gallon water and methanol tank.

Fuel capacity
6,000 gallons contained in four self-sealing tanks in each wing.

Payload
Combinations of: vehicles, artillery, dismantled aircraft etc, as dictated by weight and/or physical size. Alternatively, as a personnel carrier: 70 Paratroops (30 in tail boom/40 in freight hold), 94 fully equipped troops (36 in tail boom/58 in freight hold), and 48 stretcher casualties in the freight hold - with 34 non-stretcher casualties in the tail boom.

Beverley serial allocations were:
XB259 – XB269
XB283 – XB291
XH116 – XH124
XL117 – XL119 (Renumbered – XL130 – XL132)
XL148 – XL152
XM103 – XM112

Above and below: Beverley XB259, RAE seen at RAF Wildenrath, Germany, March 1968. 'The First (to fly) And The Last (to fly)'. A play on words but factually correct as related in the Beverley's introduction. Two views showing XB259 minus clamshell doors but with baffle plates fitted, a few months after the retirement of RAF operated Beverleys. The paint scheme shown was adopted in 1966 and comprised gloss white overall with orange Day-Glo nose, wingtip under surfaces (possibly not the upper surfaces though!), outer surfaces of the vertical tail and propeller spinners. Control surfaces remained gloss white. Gloss black was applied to fuselage under surfaces, the anti-glare panel in front of the cockpit and engine nacelles, although the starboard inner cowling is apparently natural metal; whether or not this applied to the port inner also, or whether it is a replacement cowling is not clear.

Above: Beverley XB267 'B', 47 Squadron, location not stated but possibly RAF Abingdon, July or August 1964. First flown on 30th December 1955, this aircraft was issued to 47 Squadron in March 1956 and subsequently transferred to 53 Squadron, remaining with that unit until the latter merged with 47 Squadron; XB267 thus reverted to its original user. By November 1967, the Beverley was at 27MU awaiting disposal and was sold for scrap on 25th September 1969. Orange Day-Glo has been applied, so presumably, this aircraft was allocated for training purposes, perhaps – and it is by no means certain, following repairs to damage caused to XB267 earlier in 1964. The aircraft was repaired at Abingdon. Of note is the Squadron Motif, rendered differently to other styles that appear in this section and, on the extreme left of this image, a 'Giraffe'; a platform designed to allow access to such lofty installations as the engines for instance.

Below: Beverley XB285 'C', 47 Squadron, at the Rolls-Royce airfield, Hucknall, 12th May 1964. First flown on 25th May 1956 and delivered to 47 Squadron on 6th June 1956, coded 'J'. This aircraft spent six months with the A&AEE from April 1963, to test updated avionics and, on return to 47 Squadron, was recoded 'C', following which in September 1964, it returned once more for another period with the A&AEE, returning to Abingdon the following July. On 19th October 1967, XB285 was dispatched to 71 MU and sold for scrap on 8th January 1969.

Opposite page top: Beverley XB287 'T', date and location unknown. First flown on 4th July 1956, this aircraft went first to 53 Squadron on the 24th of the month coded 'T' and, other than returning to the manufacturer, remained with the same unit until it merged with 47 Squadron in 1963, by whom it was retained. On 7th October 1966, XB287 was loaned to 84 Squadron for a month before returning to the UK and its parent unit on 6th November. On 10th November 1967, XB287 arrived at 27 MU and sold for scrap on 27th September 1969.

Opposite page bottom and this page top: Beverley XB288 'U'. Dates and locations unknown. First flown on 3rd August 1956, this aircraft joined 53 Squadron just three days later coded 'U', joining 47 Squadron after the two units merged. On 19th October 1967, XB288 arrived at 71 MU and was sold for scrap on 8th January 1969 to a scrap merchant in Buckinghamshire where, 20 years later its hulk still remained. The non-flying image shows XB288 in the company of other Beverleys and at least six examples of the Armstrong Whitworth (later, Hawker Siddeley) Argosy. The 47 Squadron Motif appears to be of a later form than those displayed in the photograph shown opposite bottom.

Above: Beverley XL131 'L', 47 Squadron, RAF West Raynham, Norfolk, 16th July 1965. This aircraft was originally to have received the serial XL118, however this was subsequently altered to XL131 and as such was first flown on 23rd May 1957 and issued to 30 Squadron during the following August, coded initially as 'J' and later 'C'. On 1st May 1964, this aircraft was transferred to 47 Squadron and recoded as 'L'. By 19th October 1967, it was with 71 MU, where it remained until 29th August 1969, when it was sold for scrap. Earlier in its career, on 22nd September 1961, XL131 had suffered an in-flight explosion whilst en-route to Bahrain in the hands of an 84 Squadron crew. The explosion was caused by a time bomb that had been planted in the hold whilst the aircraft was being loaded in Kuwait, and resulted in a large hole being blown out of the starboard fuselage just above the nose wheel. The aircraft was too badly damaged for local resources to repair and so XL131 was flown to Brough for repair by the manufacturers, having first received a temporary plywood and linen 'patch' for the journey to the UK. Once repaired, the Beverley returned to 30 Squadron on 13th July 1962.

This page and opposite: Beverley XB290 'X', 47 Squadron, RAF Waddington, 19th September 1964. First flown on 7th September 1956, this aircraft was delivered to 53 Squadron on 2nd October 1956 and coded 'W'. On 14th June 1962 XB290 was transferred to 242 OCU retaining the code 'W' and, following its service with the OCU was dispatched for modifications in May 1963, on completion of which the aircraft was transferred to 47 Squadron on 1st October 1963 coded 'X'. XB290 was sent to 27 MU on 6th December 1967 and was one of the two aircraft to participate in the farewell flypast over Upavon on that

day. XB290 was sold for scrap on 25th March 1970. The images featuring Day-Glo are dated 19th September 1964, at which time the Squadron crane Motif, displayed on the fins, possessed a bold style without a background. Those images lacking Day-Glo, show the Motif in an alternative, perhaps later form which would therefore suggest a later date, although doubtless, for a while both styles would have been in use simultaneously. Whatever the veracity of the dating evidence may be, it is worth noting that the crane's beak points to the rear on the starboard fin and forward on the port fin.

This page and opposite page: Beverley XM111 'D', 47 Squadron, Hucknall, date unknown. XM111 first flew on 19th April 1958 and was the penultimate Beverley built. On 15th July 1958 this aircraft was delivered to 84 Squadron but was then loaned almost immediately to the Abingdon Wing for nearly two months before being returned on 9th September, at which time XM111 was coded 'W'. Apart from periods with the manufacturer or 27 MU, the Beverley remained with 84 Squadron until 7th September 1965 when it was delivered to 32 MU for refurbishment and the application of the camouflage scheme seen here, after which it was assigned to 47 Squadron on 24th November 1965, coded 'D'. On 4th January 1967, the aircraft was transferred abroad to 30 Squadron until 21st July when it returned once again to 84 Squadron, still coded 'D'. By 13th November 1967, XM111 was with 27 MU and sold for scrap on 29th August 1969. The images seen here show XM111 displaying the 47 Squadron Badge whilst in the UK, so, although the date is not recorded, it can be narrowed down to the period between November 1965 and January 1967, so probably the summer of 1966. Of interest is the fact that XM111 was one of the last three Beverleys to fly out of Aden on 6th November 1967, XL130 and XM103 being the other two. It was an eventful journey. Whilst flying over the Red Sea, XM111 became the victim of a double engine failure whilst heavily loaded and had little choice other than to divert to Jeddah, followed by XL130 in order to provide whatever assistance they could to the crew of the disabled aircraft. Having landed, the crew of XL130 were ordered to leave at gunpoint; the Saudi authorities were, at that time, very anti-British. XL130 resumed its flight only to be intercepted later by Egyptian MiG fighters near to the Egyptian coast, whose pilots fired either warning shots with rockets and cannon fire toward the Beverley, or, were incredibly poor shots and missed! This was despite the earlier submitted flight plan. Pilot and crew survived unhurt and XL130 carried on. Ultimately, the crew of XM111 were able to repair one of the two failed engines whilst awaiting a replacement for the other, which was delivered by an Argosy.

Opposite page top: Beverley XL149 'X' ex-84 Squadron, RAF Finningley, 17th September 1969. First flown on 15th July 1957 and issued to 242 OCU on 1st November 1957 where it received the code 'X' and which it retained for the remainder of its life. On 28th October 1964, this aircraft was sent to 32 MU, RAF St.Athan, to receive an application of camouflage and a general refurbishment, following which XL149 was issued to 84 Squadron on 8th February 1965, remaining with this unit until transferred to 30 Squadron on 14th August 1967. Just over a month later, it was dispatched to 27 MU where it had arrived by 18th September, awaiting disposal. However, XL149 was reprieved and moved to Finningley on 6th November 1967 for use as a ground instructional airframe and received the Maintenance serial 7988M. The Beverley remained there until broken up in 1977.

Opposite page bottom: A close up image of 84 Squadron's distinctive motif, not always rendered in such a gory fashion, often simply depicting the black scorpion without embellishment. The scorpion represents the squadron's long association with operating in areas in which scorpions are commonly found, consequently the arachnid was incorporated into the Squadron Badge, their motto 'scorpiones pungunt' i.e. 'scorpion's sting'. Contained within the body of the scorpion is the silhouette of a Wessex helicopter that bears the number '72'. In August 1964 72 Squadron re-equipped with the Westland Wessex HC.2, but the specific connection between 72 and 84 Squadrons remains unknown to the author – could it be a 'zap'?

Below: The end is nigh! XM108 seen at 27 MU RAF Shawbury, where it had been received on 8th September 1967 and eventually sold for scrap on 23rd of March 1970. This aircraft had first flown on 5th February 1958 and was delivered to 84 Squadron in the following May coded 'T'. XM108 remained with this Squadron receiving its camouflage scheme in late 1965 still coded 'T', but on 20th July 1967 was transferred to 30 Squadron. To the rear is Beverley 'R' its serial number cannot be distinguished but the aircraft is very possibly XM109 which had been coded 'R' from 21st November 1966 whilst serving with 84 Squadron. XM109 arrived at 27 MU on 18th September 1967, and was sold for scrap on 25th March 1970. Of note when comparing the two images of XL149 and XM108 it will be seen that the black 'heart' depicted on the tail of XM108 is inverted.

Foreign visitors to Britain

Above: Boeing Superfortress KB-50J tanker conversion, Langar, Nottinghamshire, 7th July 1962, believed to be from the 420th Air Refueling Squadron RAF Sculthorpe, Norfolk. Note the two J47-GE-23 jet engines in underwing pods, two 700 US gallon tanks under the wingtips and all armament deleted. The last seven KB-50Js based in the United Kingdom left Sculthorpe to return to the USA on 22nd March 1964.

Top: Sikorsky HRS-3 (Bu130228) rescue helicopter on board an unidentified US warship, possibly a cruiser, seen at Portsmouth, date unknown. It is apparently unusual in being painted Insignia Red rather than International Orange!

Centre: Royal Danish Air Force Douglas C-47A K-683 at RAF Waddington, 15th September 1962. The type was withdrawn from RDAF service in the 1980s.

Above: French Air Force C-47 on a visit to the UK, date and location unknown.

Top: Royal Canadian Air Force Canadair Sabre seen at Langar 7th July 1962.

Centre: RCAF Sabres at Prestwick, Ayrshire, in April 1963.

Above: SAAB J29 Tunnan, date and location unknown, although the author remains unaware of any visits to the United Kingdom by this type of aircraft whilst in Swedish service.